# THE POP PIANO PLAY

# YOU'VE GOT A FRIEND

## ... AND 12 OTHER CLASSIC POP SONGS

ARRANGED AND PERFORMED BY JOHN KEMBER

FABER *ff* MUSIC

# CONTENTS

© 2010 by Faber Music Ltd
This edition first published in 2010
Bloomsbury House 74–77 Great Russell Street London WC1B 3DA
Music processed by Jeanne Roberts
Cover design by Lydia Merrills-Ashcroft
CD recorded and produced by Porcupine Studios
Printed in England by Caligraving Ltd
All rights reserved

ISBN10: 0-571-53434-1
EAN13: 978-0-571-53434-0

To buy Faber Music publications or to find out about the full range of titles available
please contact your local music retailer or Faber Music sales enquiries:

Faber Music Ltd, Burnt Mill, Elizabeth Way, Harlow CM20 2HX
Tel: +44 (0) 1279 82 89 82    Fax: +44 (0) 1279 82 89 83
sales@fabermusic.com    fabermusic.com

# PREFACE

The *Pop Piano Player* books aim to help pianists understand and play a
selection of the greatest pop songs so that they are truly 'under their fingers'.
The pieces in this book span almost five decades of popular music, representing styles
from the 60's to the present day and from musicians from both sides of the Atlantic.

Each piece is presented in two formats, which gives both the basic chord structure
and symbols as well as a piano arrangement of each song. By learning the changes,
the chords will become familiar, the progressions more readily understood and the
shapes will lie more comfortably under the hands. More information on how to interpret
and voice the chords is given on page 72.

The first version of each song gives the melody, lyrics and chord symbols in its
standard key. Lyrics are given so that the character of each song is understood,
but all verses are not always given, depending on the length and complexity of the song.
The chord symbols enable pianists to accompany singers and instrumentalists, creating
their own style of accompaniment. This format ultimately gives pianists the foundation
on which to develop personal interpretation and improvisation.

The arrangements for solo piano which follow keep largely to the same chord patterns
though with some changes to the overall structure regarding verses etc., to create
a balanced piano solo. These solos I have recorded on the accompanying CD.

I wish to thank David Sams and Gareth Bucket for their enthusiasm and encouragement
throughout the development of this series, and in particular John Caudwell
for his expertise and advice in fine-tuning the chords

*John Kember*

# DAYDREAM BELIEVER
## (MELODY, LYRICS AND CHORD CHANGES)

Words and Music
by John Stewart

Oh! what can it mean To a day-dream be-liev-er And a home-com-ing

**Last time D.S. and fade**

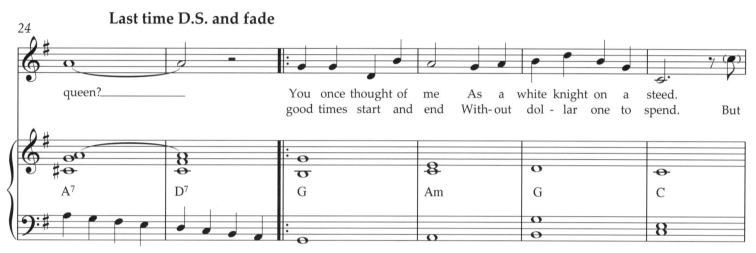

queen?

You once thought of me As a white knight on a steed.
good times start and end With-out dol-lar one to spend. But

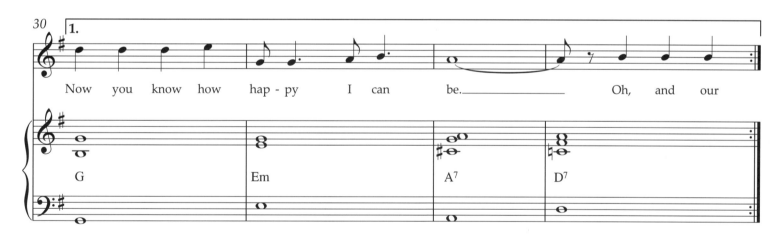

**1.**

Now you know how hap-py I can be. Oh, and our

**D. S. then repeat and fade**

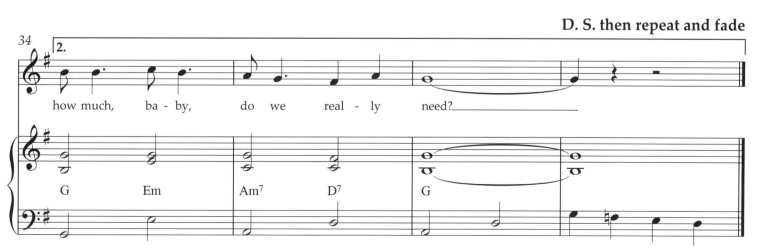

**2.**

how much, ba-by, do we real-ly need?

# DAYDREAM BELIEVER
(SOLO ARRANGEMENT)

# HELLO
## (MELODY, LYRICS AND CHORD CHANGES)

Words and Music by
Lionel Richie

# HELLO
## (SOLO ARRANGEMENT)

# PERFECT DAY

## (MELODY, LYRICS AND CHORD CHANGES)

Words and Music by
Lou Reed

# PERFECT DAY

## (SOLO ARRANGEMENT)

# RULE THE WORLD
## (MELODY, LYRICS AND CHORD CHANGES)

Words and Music by Gary Barlow, Jason Orange, Howard Donald and Mark Owen

TRACK 4

# RULE THE WORLD
## (SOLO ARRANGEMENT)

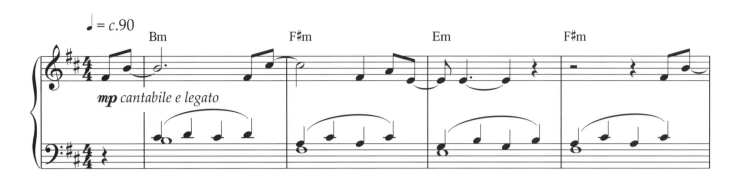

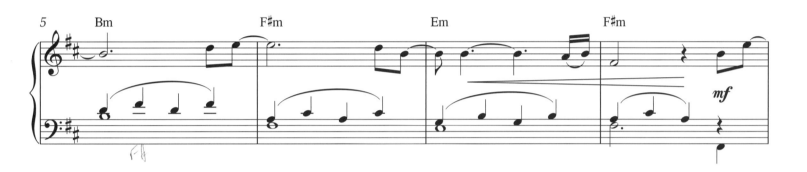

**2nd time to Coda**

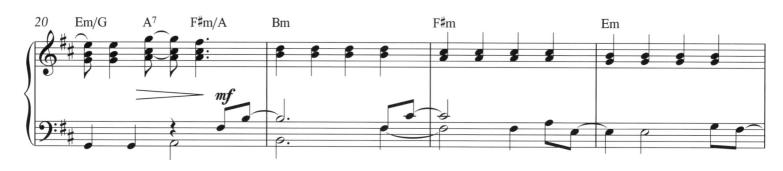

**CODA**

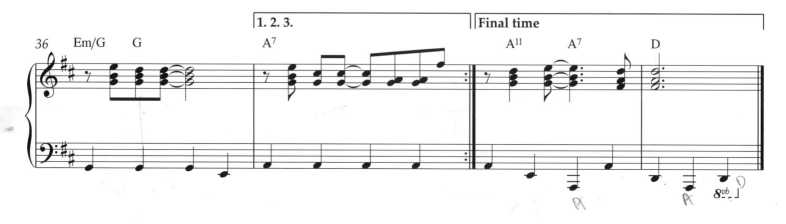

# CAN'T TAKE MY EYES OFF YOU

(MELODY, LYRICS AND CHORD CHANGES)

Words and Music by
Bob Crewe and Bob Gaudio

D. S. al Coda (3rd time)

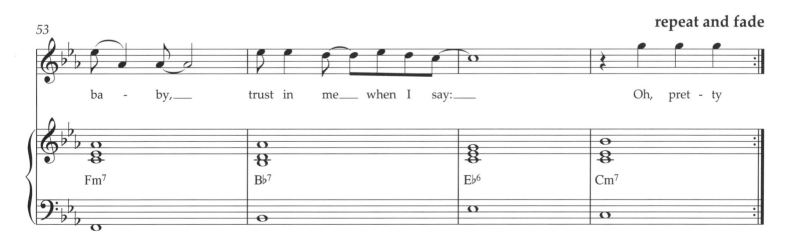

# CAN'T TAKE MY EYES OFF YOU

(SOLO ARRANGEMENT)

# THE CLIMB
## (MELODY, LYRICS AND CHORD CHANGES)

Words and Music by
Jessica Alexander and Jon Mabe

Some-times I'm gon-na have to lose. Ain't a-bout how fast I get there.

F#m¹¹     E

Ain't a-bout what's wait-ing on the o-ther side.

C#m     B⁶

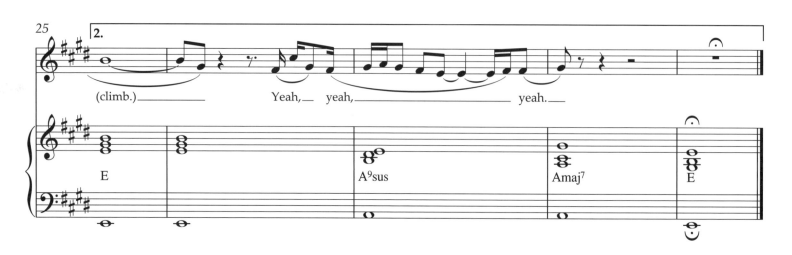

It's the climb.

Amaj⁹     A     E

(climb.) Yeah, yeah, yeah.

E     A⁹sus     Amaj⁷     E

TRACK 6

# THE CLIMB
## (SOLO ARRANGEMENT)

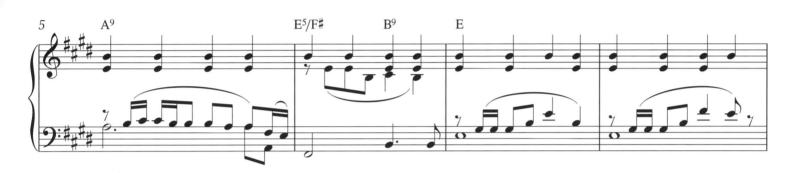

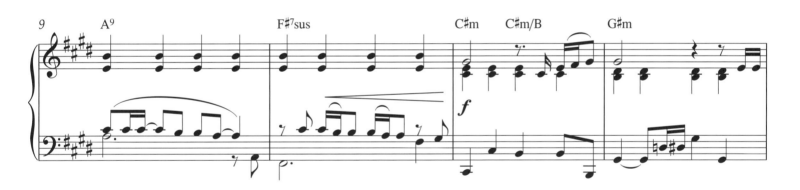

# YOU'VE GOT A FRIEND

(MELODY, LYRICS AND CHORD CHANGES)

Words and Music
by Carole King

TRACK 7

# YOU'VE GOT A FRIEND
## (SOLO ARRANGEMENT)

# YOU ARE THE SUNSHINE OF MY LIFE

(MELODY, LYRICS AND CHORD CHANGES)

Words and Music by
Stevie Wonder

# YOU ARE THE SUNSHINE
# OF MY LIFE

(SOLO ARRANGEMENT)

**Repeat (ad lib.) and fade**

# CARELESS WHISPER
## (MELODY, LYRICS AND CHORD CHANGES)

Words and Music by
George Michael and Andrew Ridgeley

# CARELESS WHISPER

(SOLO ARRANGEMENT)

# THE GREATEST LOVE OF ALL

## (MELODY, LYRICS AND CHORD CHANGES)

Words by Linda Creed
Music by Michael Masser

# THE GREATEST LOVE OF ALL
## (SOLO ARRANGEMENT)

# NOBODY DOES IT BETTER

from *The Spy Who Loved Me*

(MELODY, LYRICS AND CHORD CHANGES)

Music by Marvin Hamlisch
Lyrics by Carole Bayer Sager

# NOBODY DOES IT BETTER

from *The Spy Who Loved Me*

(SOLO ARRANGEMENT)

# TOUCH ME IN THE MORNING
## (MELODY, LYRICS AND CHORD CHANGES)

Words by Ron Miller
Music by Michael Masser

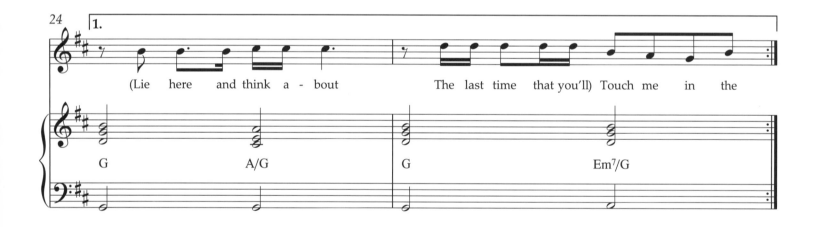

# TOUCH ME IN THE MORNING
## (SOLO ARRANGEMENT)

# I WANT YOU BACK
## (MELODY, LYRICS AND CHORD CHANGES)

Words and Music by Alphonso Mizell, Frederick Perren,
Deke Richards and Berry Gordy Jr

TRACK 13

# I WANT YOU BACK

(SOLO ARRANGEMENT)

# A CHORD GUIDE FOR POP PIANISTS

Chords in popular music tend to be mainly root based – so a chord of C major will have C as its bass (lowest note), and the 3rd and 5th notes of the scale make up the rest of the chord. The chords in pop songs are likely to revolve around just a few chosen chords, generally with one chord per bar, and frequently have a familiar or repetitive pattern. These have often been developed from the guitar rather than the keyboard.

- **Major and minor tonalities:** plain symbols such as G, D, and A denote a major chord. Minor chords are symbolised by a small 'm' as in Gm, Dm and Am. **Additional notes** can be added and are referred to as the note number above the root, such as 6th, 7th, 9th, 11th and 13th.

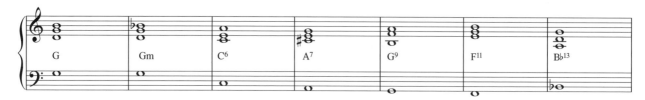

- **The major 7th** uses the seventh note of the scale named by the chord, so Dmaj7 would have a C♯. D7 implies a **minor seventh** so would have a C♮.

- The **5th can be augmented** (enlarged) by a semitone which is indicated by a ♯ or + sign, or **diminished** (reduced) by a semitone, indicated by the ♭ or − sign.

- **9ths, 11ths and 13ths** can be augmented or diminished in the same way.

- **Inverted chords** (where the bass note is other than the root) are indicated as F/A, an F major chord over an A bass, or Am/D, an A minor chord over a D bass.

- **The diminished 7th** (dim7) is made up of minor 3rd intervals to make a chord that is distinctive in tone and often used as a chromatic link between chords. The **half-diminished chord** is shown as Em7♭5 and is best thought of as Gm/E.

- The **suspended chord** (Fsus4, or just Fsus) has a fourth intending to resolve onto the third, and as such has no tonality until it does so.